cupcakes

cupcakes

whitecap

NOTES

Standard American cup measurements are used in all recipes.

1 cup = 8 fl. oz.   ½ cup = 4 fl. oz.
⅓ cup = 3 fl. oz.   ¼ cup = 2 fl. oz.

Medium eggs have been used throughout.

A few recipes include nuts or nut derivatives. It is advisable for those with known allergic reactions to nuts and nut derivatives and those who may be potentially vulnerable to these allergies, such as pregnant and nursing mothers, the elderly, babies and children, to avoid dishes made with nuts and nut oils. It is also prudent to check the labels of prepared ingredients for the possible inclusion of nut derivatives.

Ovens should be preheated to the specified temperature. If using a convection oven, follow the manufacturer's instructions for adjusting the time and temperature.

First published in Great Britain in 2004 by Hamlyn,
a division of Octopus Publishing Group Ltd
2–4 Heron Quays, London E14 4JP

This edition published in US and Canada by Whitecap Books.
For more information, contact Whitecap Books,
351 Lynn Avenue, North Vancouver, British Columbia,
Canada, V7J 2C4.

ISBN 13: 978-1-55285-626-0

ISBN 10: 1552856267

A CIP catalogue record for this book is available from the British Library

Printed and bound in China

10 9 8 7 6 5 4 3 2 1

contents

introduction

Home-made cakes are always popular with family and friends, and cupcakes are no exception. Not only are they tasty and incredibly quick and easy to make, they also give you plenty of scope for decorating. They make ideal novelty cakes for kids' parties but are equally suitable for grown-up parties and for special family occasions like Christmas, Easter, and Mother's Day.

Cupcakes keep well so you can make them in advance and keep a handy supply in the freezer or an airtight container until they're needed. If you really don't have time to make any you can even buy plain, undecorated cupcakes and decorate them yourself – within half an hour you can have a batch of beautifully presented cakes ready for guests or a hungry family.

Types of icing

Glacé icing The simplest glacé icing is simply made with confectioner's sugar and water beaten into a smooth icing. Alternatives include the use of orange or lemon juice instead of water, the addition of flavorings like instant coffee powder, or the use of coloring to tint the icing. Use a thin glacé icing to coat the top of cakes, or add more confectioner's sugar for a stiffer consistency and use it for decorative piping.

Buttercream The simplest recipe requires just confectioner's sugar and butter. Like glacé icing, it can be colored and/or flavored with ingredients such as cocoa or instant coffee powder, lemon curd, or finely grated citrus zest, and can be used both for coating the tops of cupcakes and for decorative piping. It is very simple to make but can also be bought ready-to-use.

Rolled fondant This soft and smooth, easy-to-use commercial icing is available from craft stores and cake decorating suppliers. It usually comes in white, with a subtle flavor, but like the other icings can be easily colored or flavored by kneading it with food coloring or flavoring extracts. Rolled fondant can be rolled out and cut into flat shapes or molded into fun 3D novelty decorations to be stuck on top of cakes. Knead the rolled fondant before use to warm it up, then roll it out on a surface dusted with icing sugar and move it around frequently to keep it from sticking.

Writing icing Another ready-to-use commercial icing, writing icing comes in tubes with changeable tips for piping. Ideal for fun and speedy cake decorating, it is available in a variety of colors.

Decorating cupcakes

Decorating any cake is fun, but working with cupcakes is particularly satisfying since you can produce impressive results in virtually no time at all. The various home-made or commercial icings suitable for cupcakes can be colored and used for topping the cakes, for decorative piping, or for modeling figures, but don't think such decorations restrict cupcakes to children. You can just as easily decorate cupcakes for special occasions like weddings (see page 32), or create cupcakes for a special afternoon tea party using whipped cream and thick custard as cake toppings instead of icing—see Espresso Cream Cakes (see page 58), Strawberry Cream Cakes (see page 52), and Praline Custard Cupcakes (see page 55).

There are a few decorating accessories and ingredients that you will find useful if you intend to do a lot of cupcake decorating, although you may already have some items at home.

Piping bags and tips You can buy reusable nylon piping bags and large plastic "syringes," both of which can be used with changeable tips. However, it is probably easier to use disposable paper piping bags for small-scale decorating. These can be bought ready-made from good cake decorating suppliers or you can easily make your own from triangles of parchment

paper. The advantage of disposable piping bags is that you can have several bags of icing in use at one time, whereas if you have only one reusable piping bag you will have to wash it out each time you want to change the color or type of icing you are using. The two most useful tips for decorating cupcakes are the star tip, which is used for fancy lines and star shapes, and the plain tip, which is used for lines, beads, and scribbling. Metal tips give better results than plastic ones.

Cookie cutters Made of metal or plastic, cookie cutters are invaluable for cutting out rolled fondant. They come in a variety of shapes—from simple round cutters to numerical and alphabetical shapes, animals, vehicles, hearts, stars, teddy bears, and flowers, among many others. If you cannot find a cutter with the motif that you want, simply cut out the fondant freehand with a small sharp knife. Instead of a round cookie cutter you can use an upturned glass to cut out circles.

Food coloring Food coloring is available in liquid, gel, and paste forms, and in many colors, although you can buy a few basic colors and mix them yourself to create other shades. They are quite concentrated so you need only a drop or two to color icing. Transfer the color to the icing on the end of a toothpick and mix well after each addition so that the color is evenly distributed throughout, with no streaks. You can always add more coloring but it is difficult to rectify a case of over-coloring that results in an offputting blood red or navy blue icing!

Edible cake decorations Besides the huge range of small candies suitable for decorating cupcakes—such as candy-coated chocolate drops, chocolate buttons, mini Easter eggs, gumdrops, and jelly beans—there are specialist edible decorations for cakes. Edible silver or gold balls, known as dragees, are small sugar balls with a coating of edible silver or gold leaf, while sugar strands are available in different sizes and various colors and flavors. Other specialist products include rice paper flowers, chocolate sprinkles and jimmies (both types of sugar strands), and sanding sugars (small sugar crystals). You can also buy chocolate curls or make your own by paring off "ribbons" from a bar of softened chocolate with a vegetable peeler.

½ cup (1 stick) plus 2 tablespoons **unsalted butter** or **margarine**, softened

½ cup plus 2 tablespoons **superfine sugar**

1½ cups **self-rising flour**

3 **eggs**

1 teaspoon **vanilla extract**

Vanilla cupcakes

1 Line a 12-cup muffin pan with paper baking cups. Put all the cake ingredients in a mixing bowl and beat with a hand-held electric mixer for 1–2 minutes until light and creamy. Divide the mixture evenly among the baking cups.

2 Bake in a preheated oven at 350°F for 18–20 minutes until risen and just firm to the touch. Transfer to a wire rack to cool.

Makes 12
Preparation time: 10 minutes
Cooking time: 18–20 minutes

VARIATIONS
Chocolate:
Substitute 2 tablespoons cocoa powder for 2 tablespoons of the flour.
Chocolate Chip:
Add ½ cup semisweet, milk, or white chocolate chips.
Coffee:
Add 1 tablespoon espresso or strong coffee powder.
Lemon/Orange/Citrus:
Add the finely grated zest of 1 lemon or 1 small orange, or combine the zest of ½ lemon and ½ orange.
Cranberry or Blueberry:
Add ½ cup dried cranberries or blueberries, chopped if large.
Ginger:
Add 2 teaspoons ground ginger and use light brown sugar instead of superfine sugar.
Raisin:
Add ½ cup golden raisins.

Carrot cupcakes

1 Line a 12-cup muffin pan with paper baking cups. Put the butter, sugar, flour, baking powder, apple pie spice, ground almonds, eggs, and orange zest in a mixing bowl and beat with a hand-held electric mixer for 1–2 minutes until light and creamy.

2 Add the grated carrots and golden raisins and stir into the mixture until evenly combined. Divide the mixture evenly among the baking cups.

3 Bake in a preheated oven at 350°F for 25 minutes until risen and just firm to the touch. Leave to cool in the muffin pan.

Makes 12

Preparation time: 15 minutes

Cooking time: 25 minutes

VARIATION
Banana:
Replace the grated carrots and orange zest with 1 large banana, mashed until smooth.

½ cup (1 stick) **unsalted butter** or **margarine**, softened

½ cup **light brown sugar**

1⅓ cups **self-rising flour**

1 teaspoon **baking powder**

1 teaspoon **apple pie spice**

⅓ cup **ground almonds**

2 **eggs**

finely grated zest of ½ **orange**

1¼ cups **carrots**, grated

½ cup **golden raisins**

½ cup (1 stick) plus 2 tablespoons **unsalted butter** or **margarine**, softened

½ cup plus 2 tablespoons **light brown sugar**

2 cups **self-rising flour**

3 **eggs**

1 teaspoon **almond extract**

⅓ cup **chopped mixed nuts**

½ cup **mixed dried fruit**

Fruit and nut cupcakes

1 Line a 12-cup muffin pan with paper baking cups. Put the butter, sugar, flour, eggs, and almond extract in a mixing bowl and beat with a hand-held electric mixer for 1–2 minutes until light and creamy.

2 Add the chopped nuts and dried fruit and stir in until evenly combined. Divide the mixture evenly among the baking cups.

3 Bake in a preheated oven at 350°F for 25 minutes until risen and just firm to the touch. Transfer to a wire rack to cool.

Makes 12
Preparation time: 10 minutes
Cooking time: 25 minutes

Buttercream

1 Put the butter and confectioner's sugar in a bowl and beat well with a wooden spoon or hand-held electric mixer until it is smooth and creamy.

2 Add the vanilla extract and hot water and beat again until smooth.

Makes enough to cover 12 cupcakes
Preparation time: 5 minutes

VARIATIONS
Chocolate:
Mix 2 tablespoons cocoa powder with 2 tablespoons boiling water and use instead of the vanilla extract and hot water.
Citrus:
Add the finely grated zest of 1 orange or lemon.

½ cup (1 stick) plus 2 tablespoons **unsalted butter**, softened

2 cups **confectioner's sugar**

1 teaspoon **vanilla extract**

2 teaspoons **hot water**

Cream cheese frosting

1 Beat the cream cheese in a bowl until smooth and creamy. Add the confectioner's sugar and lemon juice and beat until completely smooth.

Makes enough to cover 12 cupcakes
Preparation time: 5 minutes

4 oz. **cream cheese**

1½ cups **confectioner's sugar**

1 tablespoon **lemon juice**

Chocolate fudge frosting

3½ oz. **semisweet or milk chocolate**, chopped

2 tablespoons **milk**

¼ cup (½ stick) **unsalted butter**

¾ cup **confectioner's sugar**

1 Put the chocolate, milk, and butter in a small, heavy-based saucepan and heat gently, stirring until the chocolate and butter have melted.

2 Remove from the heat and stir in the confectioner's sugar until smooth. Spread the frosting over the tops of cupcakes while still warm.

Makes enough to cover 12 cupcakes
Preparation time: 5 minutes

White chocolate fudge frosting

7 oz. **white chocolate**, chopped

5 tablespoons **milk**

1½ cups **confectioner's sugar**

1 Put the chocolate and milk in a heatproof bowl set over a saucepan of gently simmering water and leave until melted, stirring frequently.

2 Remove the bowl from the pan and stir in the confectioner's sugar until smooth. Spread the frosting over the tops of cupcakes while still warm.

Makes enough to cover 12 cupcakes
Preparation time: 5 minutes

2–3 tablespoons **strawberry** or **raspberry jam**

12 **cupcakes** (see pages 10–12)

6 oz. **green rolled fondant**

confectioner's sugar, for dusting

4 **flaked chocolate bars**, cut into 2-inch lengths

2 oz. **red rolled fondant**

2 oz. **yellow rolled fondant**

2 oz. **white rolled fondant**

1 oz. **black rolled fondant**

Snakes in the jungle

As long as you have green icing for the cake bases, you can make the snakes any colors you like. Orange can easily be made by blending red and yellow icing, and pink by blending red and white.

1 Using a pastry brush, brush jam over the top of each cupcake. Knead the green rolled fondant on a surface lightly dusted with confectioner's sugar. Roll out very thinly and cut out 12 circles using a 2½ inch round cookie cutter. Place a green circle on top of each cake.

2 To shape a snake, take a small ball of rolled fondant—about ¼ oz.—and roll under the palm of the hand into a thin sausage about 5–6 inches long, tapering it to a point at one end and shaping a head at the other. Flatten the head slightly and mark a mouth with a small, sharp knife.

3 Thinly roll a little rolled fondant in a contrasting color and cut out small diamond shapes. Attach them along the snake using a dampened paintbrush. Wrap the snake around a length of flaked chocolate and position on top of a cupcake.

4 Make more snakes in the same way, kneading small amounts of the colored rolled fondant together to make different colors. For some of the cakes, press the chocolate bar vertically into the cake.

5 To make the snakes' eyes, roll small balls of white icing and press tiny balls of black icing over them. Secure to the snakes' heads with a dampened paintbrush.

Makes 12
Decoration time: 45 minutes

2–3 tablespoons **raspberry** or **strawberry jam**

12 **cupcakes** (see pages 10–12)

6 oz. **red rolled fondant**

confectioner's sugar, for dusting

4 oz. **black rolled fondant**

½ oz. **white rolled fondant**

small piece of **candied orange peel**, cut into matchstick lengths

Ladybugs

Thin strips of candied orange peel are used for the antennae on these little bugs. If you cannot get candied orange peel use small chocolate sticks instead.

1 Using a pastry brush, brush jam over the top of each cupcake. Knead the red rolled fondant on a surface lightly dusted with confectioner's sugar. Roll out very thinly and cut out 12 circles using a 2½ inch round cookie cutter. Place a red circle on top of each cake.

2 Roll out thin strips of black rolled fondant and position one across each red circle, securing with a dampened paintbrush. Roll out half the remaining black fondant into a thin sausage shape, about ½ inch in diameter. Cut into very thin slices and attach to the cakes to represent ladybug spots.

3 From the remaining black fondant make oval-shaped heads and secure in position. Roll small balls of the white rolled fondant for eyes and press tiny balls of black fondant over them. Attach with a dampened paintbrush.

4 To make the ladybugs' antenna, press the lengths of candied orange peel into position behind the heads, pressing small balls of black fondant onto their ends. Use tiny pieces of white fondant to shape smiling mouths.

Makes 12
Decoration time: 30 minutes

Sea monster

1 Divide the buttercream between 2 bowls. Color one half with the blue food coloring and the other with the green. Using a small offset spatula, swirl the blue buttercream over a large flat platter or tray.

2 Remove one cupcake from its paper cup and slice off the base at an angle so the top of the cake can be arranged over another at an angle to make the monster's face.

3 Spread the green buttercream over the tops of the 11 cakes in their paper cups. Place the cut cake on top of one of them and spread this with buttercream, too. Arrange the cakes on the blue buttercream base in a snaking line with the "face" cake at the front.

4 Knead the green rolled fondant on a surface lightly dusted with confectioner's sugar. Roll out 4 oz. of the fondant, keeping the rest wrapped in plastic wrap, and cut

out circles using a 3 inch round cookie cutter. Cut the circles in half and position each semicircle, upright, on the 9 center cakes. Use a little more icing to shape a small pointed tail and secure to the cake at the end.

5 For the legs, divide the reserved green fondant into 4 pieces. Shape each into a sausage, flatten the end, and cut out claw shapes. Secure around the cakes, bending them so the claws face forward.

6 Roll the green fondant trimmings and a little red fondant together until marbled. Shape some horns and attach to the monster's head. Position the gumdrops for eyes, then finish the eyes and add a mouth with a little black rolled fondant.

Makes 1 "monster" cake of 12 cupcakes
Decoration time: 20 minutes

1 quantity **Buttercream** (see page 13)

blue and **green food coloring**

12 **cupcakes** (see pages 10–12)

12 oz. **green rolled fondant**

confectioner's sugar, for dusting

½ oz. **red rolled fondant**

2 red **gumdrops**

½ oz. **black rolled fondant**

½ quantity **Buttercream** (see page 13)

12 **cupcakes** (see pages 10–12)

3½ oz. **brown rolled fondant**

confectioner's sugar, for dusting

3½ oz. **yellow rolled fondant**

3½ oz. **pink rolled fondant**

½ oz. **white rolled fondant**

½ oz. **black rolled fondant**

black food coloring

On the farm

1 Using an offset spatula, spread a thick layer of the buttercream over 4 of the cakes and lightly peak. Spread the rest of the buttercream over the remaining cakes.

2 To make the sheep, take 3 oz. of the brown rolled fondant, wrapping the remainder in plastic wrap. Knead the fondant on a surface lightly dusted with confectioner's sugar. Reserve a small piece for the ears and roll the remainder into 4 balls. Flatten each ball into an oval shape and gently press onto the cakes thickly spread with buttercream. Shape and position small ears on each sheep.

3 To make the cows, reserve a small piece of the yellow rolled fondant for the ears. Roll the remainder into 4 balls and flatten into oval shapes as large as the cake tops. Gently press onto 4 more cakes. Shape and position the ears. Use the remaining brown rolled fondant to shape the cows'

nostrils and horns, attaching with a dampened paintbrush.

4 To make the pigs, reserve 1 oz. of the pink rolled fondant for the snouts and ears. Roll the remainder into 4 balls and flatten into rounds, almost as large as each cake top. Shape and position the snouts and floppy ears, pressing 2 small holes in each snout with the tip of a toothpick or fine skewer.

5 Use the white and black fondant to make all the animals' eyes – their shape and size to suit each animal. Roll small balls of white icing and press tiny balls of black icing over them. Attach with a dampened paintbrush.

6 Use a fine paintbrush, dipped in the black food coloring, to paint on additional features.

Makes 12
Decoration time: 45 minutes

1 quantity **Buttercream** (see page 13)

blue food coloring

12 **cupcakes** (see pages 10–12)

1 oz. **blue rolled fondant**

1 oz. **red rolled fondant**

1 oz. **green rolled fondant**

2 oz. **yellow rolled fondant**

confectioner's sugar, for dusting

2 oz. **white rolled fondant**

Rainbow cakes

1 Color the buttercream with the blue food coloring and spread it all over the tops of the cupcakes using a small offset spatula.

2 To make the rainbows, take ½ oz. of the blue, red, green, and yellow fondant and roll each piece under the palms of the hands on a surface lightly dusted with confectioner's sugar until about 16 inches long. Push the strips together and then lightly roll with a rolling pin to flatten them and secure together.

3 Cut into 6 pieces, roughly 3 inches long, and attach to half the cupcakes, bending them into rainbow shapes and trimming off any excess around the edges. Reserve 1 oz. of the remaining yellow fondant, then use all the leftover colored fondant to make another 6 rainbows for the rest of the cakes in the same way.

4 Thinly roll out the white fondant and cut out little clouds. Attach to half the cakes.

5 To make the sun, thinly roll the remaining yellow icing and cut out 6 1½ inch circles. Using the tip of a sharp knife cut out little triangles from around the edges to make points. Bend the points slightly to one side and position the suns on the remaining cakes.

Makes 12
Decoration time: 25 minutes

Princess cakes

If you can find them, use silver-colored paper baking cups to make these little cupcakes even more fit for a princess.

1 Divide the buttercream between 2 bowls and add a few drops of pink food coloring to one bowl. Mix well to color the buttercream. Using a small offset spatula, spread the pink buttercream over the tops of the cupcakes to within ¼ inch of the edges, doming it up slightly in the middle.

2 Put half the white buttercream in a piping bag fitted with a plain tip and the remainder in a bag fitted with a star tip. Pipe lines, ½ inch apart, across the pink buttercream, then across in the other direction to make a diamond pattern.

3 Use the buttercream in the other bag to pipe little stars around the edges. Decorate the piped lines with silver dragees.

Makes 12
Decoration time: 20 minutes

1 quantity **Buttercream** (see page 13)

pink food coloring

12 **cupcakes** (see pages 10–12)

edible silver dragees

1 quantity **Buttercream** (see page 13)

green or **yellow food coloring**

12 **cupcakes** (see pages 10–12)

6 oz. **white rolled fondant**

confectioner's sugar, for dusting

2 oz. **red rolled fondant**

2 oz. **blue rolled fondant**

colored **sugar strands**

Number cakes

These are quick and easy and a great party cake for younger children. You can cut out the numbers by hand using a sharp knife, or use small number cookie cutters. The numbers could simply run from 1 to 12, or could represent the ages of the party goers.

1 Color the buttercream with green or yellow food coloring and spread all over the tops of the cupcakes using a small offset spatula.

2 Knead the white rolled fondant on a surface lightly dusted with confectioner's sugar then roll out. Cut out 12 circles using a 2½ inch round cookie cutter and gently press one onto the top of each cake.

3 Roll out the red rolled fondant and cut out half the numbers. Attach to the cakes with a dampened paintbrush. Use the blue rolled fondant for the remaining numbers.

4 Lightly brush the edges of white fondant with a dampened paintbrush and sprinkle with the sugar strands.

Makes 12
Decoration time: 15 minutes

1 quantity **Cream Cheese Frosting** (see page 13)

12 **Carrot Cupcakes** (see page 11)

½ oz. **white rolled fondant**

3 oz. **red rolled fondant**

handful of **small multi-colored candies**

confectioner's sugar, for dusting

1 tube **green writing icing**

thin red **ribbon**, to decorate (optional)

Christmas stockings

Use any selection of the smallest candies you can find to decorate these little cakes. Alternatively, use larger, soft candies and chop them into small pieces. If you are making them for small children you might prefer to use Vanilla Cupcakes (see page 10) and spread them with Buttercream (see page 13).

1 Using a small offset spatula, spread the frosting over the tops of the cupcakes, spreading it right to the edges.

2 Roll the white rolled fondant and a tiny piece of the red rolled fondant together on a work surface under your fingers so they twist together. Cut into ¾ inch lengths and bend one end of each length to make candy canes. You'll need about 24 altogether.

3 Pile several colored candies to one side on the top of each cake and tuck the candy canes among them.

4 Knead the remaining red fondant on a surface lightly dusted with confectioner's sugar. Roll out then cut out small stocking shapes using a sharp knife, making sure the top edge of each stocking is at least 1 inch wide. Lay the stocking shapes just over the candy decorations. Use the green writing icing to pipe details onto the stockings.

5 If desired, tie a length of red ribbon around each paper baking cup to decorate and finish with a bow.

Makes 12
Decoration time: 20 minutes

Christmas garland

Make the cakes a couple of days beforehand, or well in advance and freeze them, so all you have to do is assemble the garland up to 24 hours before serving. Use gold, silver, patterned, or white paper baking cups.

1 Press the jam through a sieve into a small saucepan and add the water. Heat gently until softened then spread in a thin layer over the tops of the cupcakes.

2 Arrange 15–16 of the cakes in a staggered circle on a round flat platter or tray, at least 14 inches in diameter. Using a small fine sieve or tea strainer dust the cakes on the platter with plenty of confectioner's sugar.

3 Fold a piece of paper into quarters then cut out a holly leaf shape, about 2½ inches long. Press a holly leaf paper template gently on the center of 4 more cakes and dust lavishly with confectioner's sugar. Carefully lift off the templates by sliding a knife under the paper to remove them without disturbing the

confectioner's sugar. Repeat on the remaining cakes. Arrange the cakes in a circle on top of the first layer.

4 Cut the grapes into small clusters. Tuck all the fruit into the gaps around the cakes and into the center of the plate. Finish by arranging small sprigs of bay leaves around the fruits.

Makes 1 garland of 24 cupcakes
Decoration time: 15 minutes

6 tablespoons **apricot jam**

1 tablespoon **water**

24 **Fruit and Nut Cupcakes** (see page 12) or **Cranberry Cupcakes** (see page 10)

confectioner's sugar, for dusting

bunch of **red grapes**, washed

bunch of **green grapes**, washed

3–4 **clementines**, halved

3–4 **figs**, halved

plenty of **bay leaf sprigs**

3½ oz. **white rolled fondant**

1¾ cups **confectioner's sugar**, plus extra for dusting

12 **cupcakes** (see pages 10–12)

½ quantity **Buttercream** (see page 13)

4–5 teaspoons **cold water**

¼ cup **shredded, unsweetened coconut**

Christmas stars

These festive cakes look stunning on the Christmas dessert table. If you have time, make the stars at least 2 hours in advance so they firm up before you decorate the cakes.

1 Knead the white rolled fondant on a surface lightly dusted with confectioner's sugar. Roll out thickly and cut out star shapes using a small, star-shaped cookie cutter. Transfer to a baking sheet lined with parchment paper and leave to harden while decorating the cakes.

2 Using a small sharp knife, cut out a deep, cone-shaped center from each cake. Fill the cavity in each cake with buttercream and position the cut-out cones on each with the crust side face down.

3 Mix the confectioner's sugar in a bowl with the cold water until smooth—the icing should hold its shape but not be too firm. Carefully spread the icing over the cupcakes and sprinkle with the coconut.

4 Gently press a star into the top of each cake and allow to set.

Makes 12
Decoration time: 25 minutes

12 **Fruit and Nut Cupcakes**
(see page 12)

4 tablespoons **brandy** or
orange-flavored liqueur
(optional)

2–3 tablespoons **apricot jam**

1 cup **ground hazelnuts** or
almonds

¼ cup **superfine sugar**

2 cups **confectioner's sugar**,
plus extra for dusting

yellow food coloring

1 tablespoon **egg white**

4–5 teaspoons **cold water**

1 oz. **green rolled fondant**

1 oz. **red rolled fondant**

Mini Christmas cakes

1 Drizzle the cupcakes with the liqueur, if using. Spread ½ teaspoon jam on the center of each cake.

2 To make the marzipan, put the ground nuts, superfine sugar, ½ cup of the confectioner's sugar, and a few drops of yellow food coloring in a bowl. Add the egg white and mix with a round-bladed knife until the mixture starts to cling together. Finish mixing the paste by hand until smooth and very firm. Lightly knead the marzipan and shape into a thick sausage, 3½ inches long. Cut into 12 thin slices and place a slice on top of each cake.

3 Put the remaining confectioner's sugar in a bowl and add the cold water to make a thick smooth paste—the icing should hold its shape but not feel too firm. Gently spread the icing over the marzipan.

4 Use the green and red rolled fondant to make small holly leaves and berries. Use to decorate the tops of the cakes.

Makes 12

Decoration time: 30 minutes

Love hearts

Make these as a family treat for Valentine's Day. Use Cream Cheese Frosting (see page 13) or White Chocolate Fudge Frosting (see page 14) instead of the glacé icing if preferred.

1 Put the confectioner's sugar in a bowl and add 4 teaspoons of the rosewater or lemon juice. Mix until smooth, adding a little more liquid if necessary, until the icing is a thick paste. Spread over the tops of the cupcakes.

2 Knead the red rolled fondant on a surface lightly dusted with confectioner's sugar. Roll out thickly and cut out 12 heart shapes using a small heart-shaped cookie cutter. Place a heart on top of each cake.

3 Press the jam through a small sieve to remove any seeds or pulp. Put the sieved jam in a small piping bag fitted with a plain tip. Pipe small dots onto the icing around the edges of each cake and pipe a line of jam around the edges of the hearts.

Makes 12
Decoration time: 20 minutes

1¾ cups **confectioner's sugar**

4–5 teaspoons **rosewater** or **lemon juice**

12 **cupcakes** (see pages 10–12)

3½ oz. **red rolled fondant**

confectioner's sugar, for dusting

6–8 tablespoons **strawberry jam**

12 **Vanilla Cupcakes** (see page 10)

4 tablespoons **sherry** or **orange-flavored liqueur** (optional)

1¾ cups **confectioner's sugar**, sifted

1–2 tablespoons **lemon juice**

36 **candy almonds**

12 **frosted flowers** (see page 43)

thin white **ribbon**, to decorate

Wedding cupcakes

Prettily decorated with candy almonds, these little cakes are perfect for a country-style family wedding. You could add guests' name tags to them and place them around the dining table. Choose candy almonds to suit the color scheme of the wedding. If using ribbon, secure it around the baking cups before you begin decorating.

1 Drizzle the cakes with the liqueur, if using. Mix the confectioner's sugar in a bowl with 1 tablespoon of the lemon juice. Gradually add the remaining lemon juice, stirring well with a wooden spoon until the icing holds its shape but is not difficult to spread—you might not need all the juice.

2 Spread the lemon-flavored icing over the tops of the cupcakes using a small offset spatula and arrange 3 sugared almonds in the center of each.

3 Place a frosted flower on top of each cake and tie a length of white ribbon around each paper baking cup to decorate it, finishing it with a bow.

Makes 12
Decoration time: 20 minutes

1 quantity **Chocolate Buttercream** (see page 13) or **Chocolate Fudge Frosting** (see page 14)

12 **Chocolate Cupcakes** (see page 10)

7 oz. **flaked chocolate bars**, cut into 1-inch lengths

36 candy-covered **mini chocolate eggs**

Easter nests

1 Using a small offset spatula, spread the buttercream or chocolate icing over the tops of the cupcakes, spreading the mixture right to the edges.

2 Cut the short lengths of flaked chocolate bars lengthways into thin "shards."

3 Arrange the chocolate shards around the edges of the cakes, pressing them into the icing at different angles to resemble birds' nests. Pile 3 eggs into the middle of each "nest."

Makes 12
Decoration time: 20 minutes

1 quantity **Buttercream** (see page 13)

yellow and **blue food coloring**

12 **cupcakes** (see pages 10–12)

2 **maraschino cherries**

Ducks, bunnies, and chicks

1 Put two-thirds of the buttercream in a bowl, beat in a few drops of yellow food coloring and mix well. Using a small offset spatula, spread the yellow icing in a flat layer over the tops of the cakes.

2 Color the remaining buttercream with blue food coloring. Place in a piping bag fitted with a plain tip, or use a parchment paper piping bag with the tip snipped off.

3 Pipe simple duck, bunny, and chick shapes onto the iced cupcakes. Cut the cherries into thin slices, then into tiny triangles and use to represent beaks on the ducks and chicks, and tiny eyes on the bunnies.

Makes 12
Decoration time: 25 minutes

2½ cups **confectioner's sugar**

2 tablespoons **cold water**

black and **red food coloring**

12 **cupcakes** (see pages 10–12)

12 **gummy insects**

Spiders' webs

For best results, finish decorating one cake before moving on to the next as the icing must be really soft to make the web patterns work well. Use any selection of sweet insects—either the spiders or the bugs can be caught in the web!

1 Beat the confectioner's sugar in a bowl with the cold water until smooth—the icing should be soft enough to lose its shape when the spoon is lifted from the bowl. If necessary add a dash more water.

2 Transfer one-fourth of the icing to a separate bowl and stir in a little black food coloring. Put in a piping bag fitted with a plain tip.

3 Color the remaining icing red. Drop 1 teaspoonful of the red icing onto a cake and spread it to the edges. Starting at the edges of the cake, pipe a spiral of black icing that finishes in the center of the cake. Run the tip of a toothpick or fine skewer from the center of the spiral out to the edge. Repeat at intervals around the cake to make a spider's web pattern, then decorate with a gummy insect.

4 Repeat on all the remaining cupcakes.

Makes 12
Decoration time: 25 minutes

Flying bats

1 Knead the black rolled fondant on a surface lightly dusted with confectioner's sugar. Roll out thickly and cut out 12 bat shapes by hand or using a small bat-shaped cookie cutter. Transfer to a baking sheet lined with parchment paper and leave to harden while decorating the cakes.

2 Spread ½ teaspoon honey over the top of each cupcake. Thinly roll out the orange rolled fondant and cut out circles using a 2½ inch round cookie cutter. Place an orange circle on top of each cake.

3 Place a bat on top of each cake. Dampen the edge of the orange fondant and press the candies gently into the icing. Pipe a wiggly line of black icing over the sweets.

Makes 12
Decoration time: 30 minutes

4 oz. **black rolled fondant**

confectioner's sugar, for dusting

2–3 tablespoons **clear honey**

12 **cupcakes** (see pages 10–12)

6 oz. **orange rolled fondant**

1 tube **black writing icing**

selection of tiny red, orange, and yellow **candies**

12 **Vanilla Cupcakes** (see page 10)

1 quantity **Buttercream** (see page 13)

Butterfly cakes

1 Using a small, sharp knife cut out the center from each cake and slice each scooped-out piece in half.

2 Put the buttercream in a big piping bag fitted with a large star tip. Pipe a large swirl of icing into the hollow of each cake.

3 Reposition the cut-out centers on each cake at an angle of 45° so they resemble butterfly wings.

Makes 12
Decoration time: 15 minutes

7 tablespoons **raspberry** or **strawberry jam**

12 **Orange Cupcakes** (see page 10)

2½ cups **confectioner's sugar**

2–3 tablespoons **orange juice**

Feather cakes

For these delicately patterned cakes, finish decorating one cake before starting on another as the icing quickly starts to set once spooned onto the cakes.

1 Press the jam through a sieve to remove any seeds or pulp. Put 3 tablespoons of the sieved jam into a small piping bag fitted with a plain tip and set aside. Spread the remaining jam over the tops of the cupcakes.

2 Put the confectioner's sugar in a bowl and beat in the orange juice until smooth—the icing should be soft enough to lose its shape when the spoon is lifted from the bowl. If necessary add a few more drops of juice.

3 Spoon a thick layer of icing onto a cake and spread it to the edges. Using the jam in the piping bag, pile large dots of jam, ½ inch apart, onto the icing in a spiral, working from the edge of the cake to the center. Draw the tip of a toothpick or fine skewer through the dots so they almost join up.

4 Repeat on the remaining cakes and leave to set.

Makes 12
Decoration time: 15 minutes

Frosted primrose cakes

These make a great gift for Mom—on Mother's Day or at any time during spring when flowers like primroses are at their best. Once frosted, the flowers keep for several weeks in a cool place so you can make them well in advance.

1 Make sure the flowers are clean and thoroughly dry before frosting. Put the egg white in a small bowl and the sugar in another.

2 Using your fingers or a soft brush, coat all the petals on both sides with egg white. Dust plenty of sugar over the flowers until evenly coated. Transfer to a sheet of nonstick baking parchment and leave for at least 1 hour until firm.

3 Using a small offset spatula, spread the chocolate frosting over the tops of the cupcakes. Decorate the top of each with the frosted flowers. Tie a length of ribbon around each paper cake case to decorate and finish in a bow.

Makes 12
Decoration time: 30 minutes

selection of small **spring flowers** such as primroses, violets or rose petals

a little lightly beaten **egg white**

superfine sugar, for dusting

1 quantity **White Chocolate Fudge Frosting** (see page 14)

12 **Vanilla Cupcakes** (see page 10)

thin pastel-colored **ribbon**, to decorate

1¾ cups **confectioner's sugar**, plus a little extra

2–3 tablespoons **lemon** or **orange juice**

12 **cupcakes** (see pages 10–12)

½ quantity **Buttercream** (see page 13)

pink and **lilac food coloring**

Piped cupcakes

These are great fun for all the family to create—children love piping their own designs and personalizing cakes with names or messages. The pink and lilac piping looks pretty on the white background but you can choose any mixture of colors you like.

1 Mix the confectioner's sugar in a bowl with 1 tablespoon of the lemon or orange juice. Gradually add the remaining juice, stirring well with a wooden spoon until the icing holds its shape but is not difficult to spread. You might not need all the juice.

2 Reserve 5 tablespoons of the icing and spread the remainder over the tops of the cupcakes using a small offset spatula. Stir a little extra confectioner's sugar into the reserved icing to thicken it until it just forms peaks when lifted with a knife. Put in a piping bag fitted with a plain tip.

3 Color half the buttercream with pink food coloring and the other half with lilac. Place in separate piping bags fitted with star tips.

4 Pipe rows of pink, lilac, and white icing across some of the cakes.

Makes 12
Decoration time: 30 minutes

1 quantity **Cream Cheese Frosting** (see page 13) or **Buttercream** (see page 13)

12 **cupcakes** (see pages 10–12)

selection of **small candies**, such as mini marshmallows, gumdrops, or jelly beans

Candy cakes

To make these cakes really effective stick to the same shades of color throughout for the candy decorations—either pastels or shocking colors—combining 2 or 3 different types of candies. These are great fun for children to decorate.

1 Using a small offset spatula, spread the frosting or buttercream over the tops of the cupcakes.

2 Decorate each cake by sprinkling with a thick, even layer of candies.

Makes 12
Decoration time: 10 minutes

Stars, spots, and stripes

1 Using a small offset spatula, spread the buttercream in a thin layer over the tops of the cupcakes.

2 Knead the rolled fondants on a surface lightly dusted with confectioner's sugar, keeping the colors separate. Take 2 oz. of the white fondant, roll out thinly, and cut out 4 circles using a 2½ inch round cookie cutter. Cut out 6 small stars from each circle using a tiny star-shaped cutter. Thinly roll out a little of the fondant and cut out stars. Fit the blue stars into each white round and carefully transfer to 4 of the cakes.

3 Thinly roll out another 2 oz. of the white fondant. Roll balls of blue fondant, about the size of a small pea, between the finger and thumb. Press at intervals onto the white fondant. Gently roll with a rolling pin so the blue fondant forms dots over the white. Cut out 4 circles using the round cookie cutter and transfer to 4 more of the cakes.

4 From the remaining blue and white fondant cut out long strips ¼ inch wide and lay them together on the work surface to make stripes. Roll lightly with a rolling pin to flatten them and secure together, then cut out 4 more circles. Place on top of the remaining 4 cakes.

Makes 12
Decoration time: 20 minutes

½ quantity **Buttercream** (see page 13)

12 **cupcakes** (see pages 10–12)

5 oz. **white rolled fondant**

4 oz. **blue rolled fondant**

confectioner's sugar, for dusting

7 oz. (about ½ can) **sweetened condensed milk**

¼ cup **superfine sugar**

5 tablespoons **unsalted butter**

3 tablespoons **golden syrup** or **light corn syrup**

12 **cupcakes** (see pages 10–12)

3½ oz. **semisweet chocolate**, chopped

3½ oz. **milk chocolate**, chopped

Chocolate caramel cupcakes

1 Put the condensed milk, sugar, butter, and golden syrup in a medium heavy-based saucepan and heat gently, stirring, until the sugar dissolves. Cook over a gentle heat, stirring, for about 5 minutes until the mixture turns a pale fudge color.

2 Leave to cool for 2 minutes then spoon the caramel over the top of the cupcakes.

3 Melt the semisweet and milk chocolate in separate heatproof bowls, either one at a time in the microwave or by resting each bowl over a saucepan of gently simmering water. Place a couple of teaspoons of each type of melted chocolate onto a cupcake, mixing up the colors and tap the cake on the work surface to level the chocolate.

4 Using the tip of a toothpick or fine skewer, swirl the chocolates together to marble them lightly. Repeat on the remaining cakes.

Makes 12
Cooking time: 5 minutes
Decoration time: 15 minutes

¼ cup (½ stick) **unsalted butter**

¼ cup **superfine sugar**

3 tablespoons **golden syrup** or **light corn syrup**

1 cup **crispy rice cereal**

12 **cupcakes** (see pages 10–12)

confectioner's sugar, for dusting

Caramel crisp pyramids

1 Put the butter, sugar, and golden syrup in a medium heavy-based saucepan and heat gently until the sugar dissolves. Cook the mixture for 2–3 minutes until it is pale caramel colored, stirring frequently. Immerse the base of the pan in cold water to prevent further cooking.

2 Stir in the crispy rice cereal and mix until evenly coated. Pile a little of the mixture on top of each cupcake and shape into a pyramid. Leave until cold then lightly dust the tops with confectioner's sugar.

Makes 12

Cooking time: 5 minutes

Decoration time: 10 minutes

Tee-off cakes

Golf-crazy Dads will love these little cakes, particularly if you get the children involved with the decoration. If you cannot find chocolate "golf balls," you can easily shape some out of white rolled fondant and make the golf ball-like impressions with the tip of a blunt-ended paintbrush.

1 Beat the chocolate spread or chocolate fudge frosting to soften it slightly then spread it over the tops of the cupcakes using a small offset spatula.

2 Knead the green rolled fondant on a surface lightly dusted with confectioner's sugar. Roll out thinly and cut out 12 circles using a 2 inch round cookie cutter. Place a green circle on top of each cake.

3 Use the white rolled fondant to shape 12 small golf tees. Lay one on top of each cake, attaching with a dampened paintbrush. Press a foil-wrapped chocolate golf ball into the icing, alongside the tee, to finish.

Makes 12
Decoration time: 30 minutes

½ cup **chocolate hazelnut spread** or ½ quantity **Chocolate Fudge Frosting** (see page 14)

12 **cupcakes** (see pages 10–12)

7 oz. **green rolled fondant**

confectioner's sugar, for dusting

3 oz. **white rolled fondant**

12 **foil-wrapped chocolate golf balls**

12 **Vanilla Cupcakes** (see page 10)

10 oz. small **strawberries**

⅔ cup **heavy cream**

2 teaspoons **superfine sugar**

½ teaspoon **vanilla extract**

4–6 tablespoons **redcurrant jelly**

2 tablespoons **water**

Strawberry cream cakes

1 Using a small sharp knife, scoop out the center of each cupcake to leave each cake with a deep cavity. Reserve 6 of the smallest strawberries and thinly slice the remainder.

2 Using a hand-held electric mixer, whip the cream with the sugar and vanilla extract until it holds soft peaks. Spoon a little into the center of each cake and flatten slightly with the back of the spoon.

3 Arrange the sliced strawberries, overlapping, around the edges of each cake. Halve the reserved strawberries and place a strawberry half in the center of each cake.

4 Heat the redcurrant jelly in a small heavy-based saucepan with the water until melted, then brush over the strawberries using a pastry brush. Store the cakes in a cool place until ready to serve.

Makes 12
Decoration time: 20 minutes

3 small **oranges**

½ cup **superfine sugar**

1¼ cups **water**

12 **Citrus Cupcakes** (see page 10)

Candied orange cupcakes

This recipe uses whole orange slices, including the skins. Cooked in syrup over a very low heat, they turn meltingly soft and delicious.

1 Slice the oranges as thinly as possible and discard any seeds. Put the sugar in a medium heavy-based saucepan with the water and heat very gently, stirring with a wooden spoon, until the sugar dissolves.

2 Add the orange slices and reduce the heat to its lowest setting. Cover and cook very gently for about 50–60 minutes or until the orange slices are thoroughly tender.

3 Transfer the slices to a plate using a slotted spoon and leave to cool slightly. Boil the syrup left in the saucepan until it is very thick and syrupy. Allow to cool for 5 minutes.

4 Arrange the orange slices over the cupcakes. Brush the thickened syrup over the cakes and leave to cool completely.

Makes 12

Cooking time: 50–60 minutes

Decoration time: 10 minutes

Praline custard cupcakes

When making the caramel for these cakes, watch the saucepan closely toward the end of the cooking time. You want the caramel to be deep golden in color but not too dark because the sugar will start to burn and taste bitter.

½ cup **superfine sugar**

½ cup **water**

½ cup **unblanched hazelnuts**, chopped

12 **Vanilla Cupcakes** (see page 10)

1¼ cups good-quality **creamy custard**

1 To make the caramel, put the sugar in a small heavy-based saucepan with the water. Heat gently, stirring with a wooden spoon, until the sugar dissolves. Bring to a boil and boil rapidly for about 10 minutes, until the syrup turns a golden caramel color.

2 Immediately remove the pan from the heat and immerse the base in cold water for a few seconds to prevent further cooking. Stir in the nuts and pour the mixture onto a lightly oiled large baking sheet, spreading it in a thin layer. Leave for about 20 minutes until brittle.

3 Scoop out and discard the center from each cupcake using a teaspoon. Break the nut brittle in half and place one half in a plastic bag. Tap gently with a rolling pin until the brittle is broken into small chunks. Turn out onto a plate then put the remaining brittle in the bag. Beat firmly with the rolling pin until the brittle is finely crushed.

4 Mix the crushed brittle with the custard and pile the mixture into the cupcakes. Decorate with the large pieces of brittle.

Makes 12

Cooking time: 10 minutes, plus cooling

Decoration time: 15 minutes

½ cup **flaked almonds**

⅓ cup **golden raisins**

¾ cup **maraschino cherries**, quartered

6 tablespoons **golden syrup** or **light corn syrup**

12 **cupcakes** (see pages 10–12)

2 oz. **semisweet chocolate**, broken into pieces

Florentine cupcakes

1 Mix together the flaked almonds, golden raisins, maraschino cherries, and golden syrup in a bowl. Pour the mixture out onto a greased baking sheet and spread in a thin layer. Bake in a preheated oven at 400°F for 8 minutes or until the nuts and syrup are turning golden. Remove from the oven and allow to cool slightly.

2 Break up the mixture and scatter over the cupcakes in an even layer.

3 Melt the chocolate in a heatproof bowl, either in the microwave or by resting the bowl over a saucepan of gently simmering water. Put the melted chocolate in a piping bag fitted with a plain tip. Scribble lines of chocolate across the fruit and nut topping. Leave to set.

Makes 12
Cooking time: 8 minutes
Decoration time: 10 minutes

12 **Coffee Cupcakes** (see page 10)

6 tablespoons **coffee-flavored liqueur**

1¼ cups **heavy cream**

3 oz. piece of **semisweet** or **milk chocolate**

cocoa powder, for sprinkling

Espresso cream cakes

These richly flavored cakes make a delicious treat with morning coffee. If you don't want to use the liqueur, use 6 tablespoons of strong black coffee mixed with 1 teaspoon of sugar instead.

1 Flavor the cupcakes by drizzling with 3 tablespoons of the coffee-flavored liqueur.

2 Put the remaining liqueur in a bowl with the cream and whip with a hand-held electric mixer until the cream is thickened and only just holds its shape. Using a small offset spatula, spread the cream over the tops of the cupcakes, swirling it right to the edges.

3 Using a vegetable peeler, pare off curls from the chocolate bar—if the chocolate breaks off in small, brittle shards, try softening it in the microwave for a few seconds first, but take care not to overheat and melt it. Scatter the chocolate curls over the cakes and sprinkle with a little cocoa powder. Store the cakes in a cool place until ready to serve.

Makes 12
Decoration time: 10 minutes

Chocolate truffle cakes

7 oz. **semisweet chocolate**

⅔ cup **heavy cream**

12 **Chocolate Cupcakes** (see page 10)

24 **cocoa-dusted chocolate truffles**, quartered

1 Coarsely grate 2 oz. of the chocolate and set aside. Chop the remainder into pieces.

2 Heat the cream in a small heavy-based saucepan until just beginning to bubble around the edges. Remove from the heat and add the chopped chocolate. Leave to stand for a few minutes until the chocolate has melted.

3 Turn the mixture into a bowl and leave to cool until the cream just holds its shape—you can pop it in the refrigerator for a short while but don't leave it for too long because the mixture will eventually set.

4 Using a small offset spatula, spread the chocolate cream over the tops of the cupcakes. Scatter the truffle quarters over the cakes. Sprinkle with the grated chocolate and leave the cakes in a cool place until ready to serve.

Makes 12

Decoration time: 15 minutes

3½ oz. chunky piece of **white chocolate**

1 quantity **White Chocolate Fudge Frosting** (see page 14)

12 **White Chocolate Chip Cupcakes** (see page 10)

confectioner's sugar, for dusting

White chocolate curl cakes

1 Using a vegetable peeler, pare off curls from the chocolate bar—if the chocolate breaks off in small, brittle shards, try softening it in the microwave for a few seconds first, but take care not to overheat and melt it. Set the chocolate curls aside in a cool place while frosting the cakes.

2 Using a small offset spatula, spread the fudge frosting all over the tops of the cupcakes.

3 Pile the chocolate curls on the cakes and lightly dust with confectioner's sugar.

Makes 12

Decoration time: 15 minutes

3½ oz. **white chocolate**, chopped

3½ oz. **milk chocolate**, chopped

3½ oz. **semisweet chocolate**, chopped

3 tablespoons **unsalted butter**

12 **Chocolate Cupcakes** (see page 10)

cocoa powder, for dusting

Triple chocolate cupcakes

1 Put the white, milk, and semisweet chocolate in separate bowls and add 1 tablespoon butter to each. Melt all the chocolate, either one at a time in the microwave or by placing each bowl over a saucepan of gently simmering water. Stir occasionally until melted and smooth.

2 Using a small offset spatula, spread the melted white chocolate over 4 of the cakes and sprinkle with a little cocoa powder.

3 Put 3 tablespoons of the melted milk and semisweet chocolate in separate piping bags fitted with plain tips. Spread the milk chocolate over 4 more of the cakes and pipe dots of semisweet chocolate over the milk chocolate.

4 Spread the semisweet chocolate over the 4 remaining cakes and scribble with lines of piped milk chocolate.

Makes 12
Decoration time: 20 minutes

Index

Executive Editor Sarah Ford
Managing Editor Clare Churly
Executive Art Editor Geoff Fennell
Photographer Gareth Sambidge
Food stylist Joanna Farrow